Life Lessons From

Davey and Goliath

CATHERINE MALOTKY

&

DAVID ENGELSTAD

Rutledge Hill Press™

Nashville, Tennessee

A Division of Thomas Nelson Inc.

www.ThomasNelson.com

TO OUR PARENTS

Published by Rutledge Hill Press, a Division of Thomas Nelson, Inc.,
P.O. Box 141000, Nashville, Tennessee, 37214.

Library of Congress Cataloging-in-Publication Data Available
1-4016-0082-4

Printed in Colombia
03 04 05 06 07—5 4 3 2 1

WELCOME!

Between 1960 and 1975, *Davey and Goliath* existed as three-dimensional animated television characters, starring in a show viewed by millions of children worldwide.

Sixty-five episodes and six specials were created through funding from the United Lutheran Church in America and later from the Lutheran Church in America.

Like most middle-class American kids, Davey, his dog Goliath, his sister Sally, and his best friend Jonathan face the challenges of growing up. And the values first discovered in the classic *Davey and Goliath* television show are still relevant.

Regardless of how old you are, we hope you enjoy this.

HISTORY

Now
ANYTIME
CAN be
DAVEY & GOLIATH
TIME!

1958
Franklin Clark Fry, president of the United Lutheran Church in America (ULCA), puts aside $1 million to fund production of a future television program.

1959
The ULCA contracts with Clokey Productions, Inc., headed by Gumby creators Art and Ruth Clokey to create a new children's show, *Davey and Goliath*. Scripts are written by children's book author Nancy Moore in consultation with the church.

1960
The first fifteen-minute long *Davey and Goliath* episode, "Lost in a Cave," is produced.

¡David y Goliat confundieron a los expertos! Habiendo sido planeado para niños y niñas de la escuela primaria, pruebas alrededor del mundo han demostrado que el programa apela a los niños en niveles preescolar y secundario... ¡y a los mayores que se sienten jóvenes en el corazón!

¡LOS NIÑOS ACEPTARÁN EN SUS CORAZONES A DAVID Y A SU FAMILIA!

1960–1963
Episodes of *Davey and Goliath* are given free of charge to nearly 200 television markets in North America. Translated into Spanish, Portuguese, Dutch, and Cantonese, the show also appears overseas.

1962
The ULCA merges with other Lutheran churches to form the Lutheran Church in America (LCA), which then takes over funding of the show.

1965
The first *Davey and Goliath* special, a thirty-minute Christmas show entitled "Christmas Lost and Found," airs.

1967
The LCA funds three more *Davey and Goliath* specials: "New Year Promise," "Happy Easter," and "Halloween Who-Dun-It."

Davey and Goliath

An exciting, informative and entertaining children's TV series in color.

Now! 52 quarter-hour episodes that provide first-rate, professional public service programming.

1969-1971
The LCA funds another run of episodes. Davey's friends now include Jonathan Reen and Cisco, an African-American boy and a Hispanic boy. These episodes have lessons of integration and racial tolerance, charity, and community as well as the spiritual themes of the original series.

1971
A fifth special—"School . . . Who Needs It?"—is created.

1975
The final *Davey and Goliath* special, "To the Rescue," airs.

Watch the new adventures of Davey and Goliath

1988
The LCA joins with the American Lutheran Church and the Association of Evangelical Lutheran Churches to form the Evangelical Lutheran Church in America (ELCA). The ELCA now holds all rights to *Davey and Goliath*.

1990s
Davey and Goliath is referenced in pop culture venues such as *Dead Man Walking*, *The Simpsons*, *Friends*, *Beavis and Butt-head*, *Mystery Science Theatre 3000*, and *Mad TV*.

2000
Millions of children have grown up with *Davey and Goliath*. The program has been translated into seven languages, and the show has been broadcast on every continent except Antarctica.

2002
Davey and Goliath reaches millions of fans through its enormously successful Mountain Dew ad campaign.

Jimmy helps Davey learn to play the drum for the parade, and Davey helps Jimmy build a float. However, Davey lies about taking wood from a construction site to use for the float, and this gets Jimmy into trouble.

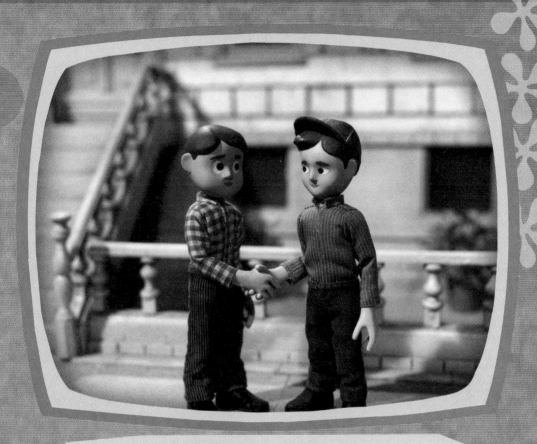

Saying "I'm sorry"
doesn't take away the hurt,
but it can start the healing.

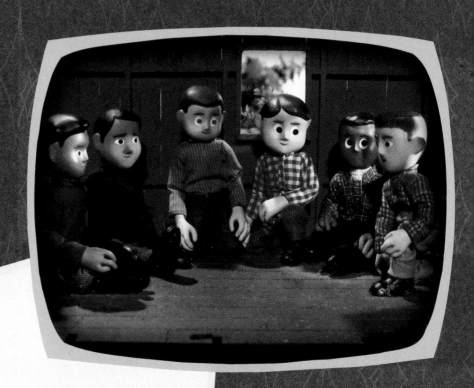

GOOD FRIENDS

lean on each other.

Even though
it's right, it's
hard to share.

Davey tries to think up a good New Year's resolution before helping Mr. Opp ring the church bell at midnight on New Year's Eve. He first chooses "Not yelling at Sally" as his resolution. He later decides that a better resolution is "Speaking nicely to Sally."

A good resolution doesn't just correct the past; it creates a future.

When we feel grateful,
we can't help but look for
opportunities to express it.

Maturity means keeping
commitments and working things out.

As Davey works with Officer Dan
on traffic patrol, he meets a boy
who is deaf. Davey learns about
deafness by wearing earplugs
and visiting a school for the deaf.

Everyone can teach us something.

NEVER

make fun of

ANYONE.

It's good to learn and respect each other's origins and customs.

Sometimes this even helps us to feel more connected to one another.

Davey's school class takes a field trip in the woods. Though their teacher warns them about wandering off, Davey and Jonathan get lost while looking for unusual leaves, bugs, and rocks.

If you learn a lesson from bad luck – that's good luck.

The best magic is when people help each other.

People are often more ready
to forgive us than we expect.

 23

The children celebrate Halloween night with a costume party and mischief making. When the mischief gets out of hand, Davey feels bad until he tells Mr. Green that he was the one who damaged the bee-hive.

TAKE RESPONSIBILITY

if it's yours to resolve.

25

When we care for the earth,
the earth cares for us.

HELPING OTHERS
is a great way to
MAKE FRIENDS.

27

Davey spends the summer at his grandparents' farm and gets excited about winning ribbons and medals at the state fair. His vegetables, however, don't grow very well because he's too busy playing to tend to them.

WISDOM BALANCES

PLAY AND WORK.

We don't have to be good at everything.

True love can forgive even foolish mistakes.

Sally and Davey got a mechanical man (a robot) named Mekano from their aunt. They learn, however, that a robot isn't the same as a real person.

Humans are miracles that love, heal, and grow.

 33

We are never really alone.

God wants us to forgive those who say, "I'm sorry."

Davey ignores the warning sign and explores an abandoned silver mine. His father helps to rescue him when falling timbers trap him inside.

Sometimes, there is no one to blame but yourself.

The unknown is the scariest.

LOVE
conquers
FEAR.

Davey is sick of life at home and runs away (for a day) to join the circus.

We all have to make our own way.

WORDS
ARE LIKE
SNOWBALLS
~

even little ones can
roll on and on
and
grow and grow.

DON'T SAY
UGLY THINGS
ABOUT PEOPLE!

Davey and his friends don't understand the foreign language of the new shoemaker in town, and decide he's mean without learning more about him.

Understanding can turn fear into friendship.

It's easy to hate a BULLY,
but even a bully needs a friend.

46

CURIOUS and CAREFUL

can go together!

 47

Life is always both

what we want to do and what we have to do.

As we think – we grow.

Davey and Jimmy work hard to build a kite. When Goliath accidentally wrecks it, they forgive him. They build another kite but get mad at Tommy when he wrecks it on purpose. They build a third kite and forgive Tommy when he says he is sorry.

We FORGIVE the people we love.

Love will help us find home again.

You can't buy forgiveness.

Davey and Sally get in a jam when
a rope bridge breaks and Sally is
stranded on a narrow ledge. Davey
remains calm and thinks of a way
to rescue her.

We can rise to the occasion.

55

God loves everyone.

Only doing the right thing is right.

Davey's dad leaves him in charge of the house. But Davey gets so busy playing with his friends that he misses the plumber's call, and the result is a big oil spill in the basement.

Responsibility means that when
you are trusted to do something,
you won't let others down.

****

You don't get good overnight.

A game of follow the leader turns
into trouble when the boys dare
each other with, "Are you chicken?"

GOD gave us our heads to use not to fall on.

It's good to think of other people's needs
and even better to do something good for them.

When we disobey someone we love – things aren't right until we say, "I'm sorry."

Davey's twin friends – Timmy and Tommy – invite him to help them set up a lemonade stand. When Davey's dad helps Sally fix her doll carriage before helping Davey build the stand, Davey feels that his dad loves Sally best.

Sometimes there is a bigger picture than we can see.

People bent on REVENGE
are no fun to be around.

You can't help everyone every time.

Sometimes you have to choose.

Davey says he hates Christmas because he doesn't feel the Christmas spirit. Buying presents, eating cookies, and listening to Christmas music don't help. But giving up something he loves for a new friend does help Davey feel the Chrismas spirit.

Christmas is really about giving.

RATIONALIZING

a poor choice won't help us feel better,
only **DOING THE RIGHT THING** will.

RULES
help us
live together.

Davey and Jonathan hunt for returnable bottles to earn money to see a movie. When they meet a boy who is doing the same to earn money for food, they share their bottles with him.

We can make a difference
when we care and work
together to help.

It pays to be a GOOD NEIGHBOR

When we feel we deserve punishment,
we hesitate to seek forgiveness.

Goliath's doghouse gets hit by lightning. Davey's father gives Davey the job of building a new one, but he doesn't think he can do it all by himself.

Sometimes we need a little push to grow.

Love makes us brave.

When we lose someone we love,
we can't replace him;
but others can help us remember.

Little things
can make
a big difference.

FORGIVE, FORGET, and START OVER.

Davey meets a new boy and his dog. When Goliath outsmarts the new boy's dog, the boy writes "Davey and Goliath" on a newly poured cement driveway. Davey gets blamed, and is so angry that all he can do is think of revenge.

REVENGE
is hard on
EVERYONE
and solves
NOTHING.

85

When we love others,
we know when they need us.

Fear of punishment clouds our thinking.

87

Davey, Teddy, and Jonathan form a band and dream of getting rich. They are offered two opportunities to play—one at the theater for money and one at a children's center for free. They choose the children's center. The sick and hurting children respond joyfully, and the boys discover that this is pay enough.

Good deeds are the best medicine.

Learning about other's disabilities sometimes

helps us appreciate our own abilities

90

The world is a DEPENDABLE MIRACLE.

God knows what we need.

Help comes in unexpected ways if we are open to it.

Scared? Play!

Sometimes being responsible means being brave.

NOTHING
is impossible with
GOD.